THIS DATING JOURNAL BELONGS TO

_____

_____

My Date with _____

DATE: _____   TIME: _____

My Favorite Things About The Date

☐

☐

☐

☐

☐

☐

Email: _____

Phone: _____

_____

Address: _____

_____

What did we do?

_____

_____

_____

Where Did we Go?

_____

_____

_____

How Much Did I Spend?

_____

_____

_____

Things We Talked About

_____

_____

_____

How Much Did my Date Spend?

_____

_____

_____

My Screw Ups

_____

_____

My Date's Screw Ups

_____

_____

Conversation from 1-10   1   2   3   4   5   6   7   8   9   10

KISSING?

IF YES
- ◯ Bad Kisser
- ◯ Mediocre Kisser
- ◯ Good Kisser

NO ◯

SEX?

IF YES, WHERE?
- ◯ My Place
- ◯ My Date's Place
- ◯ Somewhere Else

NO ◯

HOW WAS THE DATE?

- ◯ Never Again
- ◯ Awkward
- ◯ I've Had Better

- ◯ Nice
- ◯ Off the Charts
- ◯ Love at First Sight

Ideas For Next Date?

My Intentions

Notes

My Date with _____

DATE: _____   TIME: _____

My Favorite Things About The Date

☐ _____

☐ _____

☐ _____

☐ _____

☐ _____

☐ _____

Email: _____

Phone: _____

_____

Address: _____

_____

What did we do?

_____

_____

_____

Where Did we Go?

_____

_____

_____

How Much Did I Spend?

_____

_____

Things We Talked About

_____

_____

_____

How Much Did my Date Spend?

_____

_____

My Screw Ups

_____

_____

My Date's Screw Ups

_____

_____

Conversation from 1-10   1   2   3   4   5   6   7   8   9   10

KISSING?

IF YES

○ Bad Kisser

○ Mediocre Kisser

○ Good Kisser

NO ○

SEX?

IF YES, WHERE?

○ My Place

○ My Date's Place

○ Somewhere Else

NO ○

HOW WAS THE DATE?

○ Never Again

○ Awkward

○ I've Had Better

○ Nice

○ Off the Charts

○ Love at First Sight

Ideas For Next Date?

_____

_____

My Intentions

_____

_____

Notes

_____

_____

_____

_____

My Date with _____

DATE: _____   TIME: _____

My Favorite Things About The Date

☐

☐

☐

☐

☐

☐

Email: _____

Phone: _____

_____

Address: _____

_____

What did we do?

_____

_____

_____

Where Did we Go?

_____

_____

_____

How Much Did I Spend?

_____

_____

_____

Things We Talked About

_____

_____

_____

How Much Did my Date Spend?

_____

_____

_____

My Screw Ups

_____

_____

My Date's Screw Ups

_____

_____

Conversation from 1-10   1   2   3   4   5   6   7   8   9   10

⌁——♡——⌁ KISSING? ⌁——♡——⌁

IF YES
◯ Bad Kisser
◯ Mediocre Kisser
◯ Good Kisser

NO ◯

⌁——♡——⌁ SEX? ⌁——♡——⌁

IF YES, WHERE?
◯ My Place
◯ My Date's Place
◯ Somewhere Else

NO ◯

HOW WAS THE DATE?

◯ Never Again   ◯ Nice
◯ Awkward   ◯ Off the Charts
◯ I've Had Better   ◯ Love at First Sight

⌁——♡——⌁

Ideas For Next Date?

_____

_____

My Intentions

_____

Notes

_____

_____

_____

My Date with _____

DATE: _____   TIME: _____

My Favorite Things About The Date

☐

☐

☐

☐

☐

☐

Email: _____

Phone: _____

Address: _____
_____

What did we do?
_____
_____
_____

Where Did we Go?
_____
_____
_____

How Much Did I Spend?
_____
_____

Things We Talked About
_____
_____
_____

How Much Did my Date Spend?
_____
_____

My Screw Ups
_____
_____

My Date's Screw Ups
_____
_____

Conversation from 1-10   1   2   3   4   5   6   7   8   9   10

KISSING?

IF YES

○ Bad Kisser

○ Mediocre Kisser

○ Good Kisser

NO ○

SEX?

IF YES, WHERE?

○ My Place

○ My Date's Place

○ Somewhere Else

NO ○

HOW WAS THE DATE?

○ Never Again

○ Awkward

○ I've Had Better

○ Nice

○ Off the Charts

○ Love at First Sight

Ideas For Next Date?

_____

_____

My Intentions

_____

_____

Notes

_____

_____

_____

My Date with _____

DATE: _____   TIME: _____

My Favorite Things About The Date

☐

☐

☐

☐

☐

☐

Email: _____

Phone: _____

Address: _____
_____

What did we do?

_____
_____
_____
_____

Where Did we Go?

_____
_____
_____
_____

How Much Did I Spend?

_____
_____
_____

Things We Talked About

_____
_____
_____

How Much Did my Date Spend?

_____
_____
_____

My Screw Ups

_____
_____

My Date's Screw Ups

_____
_____

Conversation from 1-10   1   2   3   4   5   6   7   8   9   10

KISSING?

IF YES

O Bad Kisser

O Mediocre Kisser

O Good Kisser

NO O

SEX?

IF YES, WHERE?

O My Place

O My Date's Place

O Somewhere Else

NO O

HOW WAS THE DATE?

O Never Again   O Nice

O Awkward   O Off the Charts

O I've Had Better   O Love at First Sight

Ideas For Next Date?

_____

_____

My Intentions

_____

_____

Notes

_____

_____

_____

My Date with _____

DATE: _____   TIME: _____

My Favorite Things About The Date

☐

☐

☐

☐

☐

☐

Email: _____

Phone: _____

_____

Address: _____

_____

What did we do?

_____

_____

_____

_____

Where Did we Go?

_____

_____

_____

_____

How Much Did I Spend?

_____

_____

_____

Things We Talked About

_____

_____

_____

How Much Did my Date Spend?

_____

_____

_____

My Screw Ups

_____

_____

My Date's Screw Ups

_____

_____

Conversation from 1-10   1   2   3   4   5   6   7   8   9   10

KISSING?

IF YES

○ Bad Kisser

○ Mediocre Kisser

○ Good Kisser

NO ○

SEX?

IF YES, WHERE?

○ My Place

○ My Date's Place

○ Somewhere Else

NO ○

HOW WAS THE DATE?

○ Never Again

○ Awkward

○ I've Had Better

○ Nice

○ Off the Charts

○ Love at First Sight

Ideas For Next Date?

_____

_____

My Intentions

_____

_____

Notes

_____

_____

_____

My Date with _____

DATE: _____   TIME: _____

My Favorite Things About The Date

☐

☐

☐

☐

☐

☐

Email: _____

Phone: _____

_____

Address: _____

_____

What did we do?

_____

_____

_____

Where Did we Go?

_____

_____

_____

How Much Did I Spend?

_____

_____

_____

Things We Talked About

_____

_____

_____

How Much Did my Date Spend?

_____

_____

My Screw Ups

_____

_____

My Date's Screw Ups

_____

_____

Conversation from 1-10   1   2   3   4   5   6   7   8   9   10

KISSING?

IF YES

○ Bad Kisser

○ Mediocre Kisser

○ Good Kisser

NO ○

SEX?

IF YES, WHERE?

○ My Place

○ My Date's Place

○ Somewhere Else

NO ○

HOW WAS THE DATE?

○ Never Again

○ Awkward

○ I've Had Better

○ Nice

○ Off the Charts

○ Love at First Sight

Ideas For Next Date?

My Intentions

Notes

My Date with _____

DATE: _____　　　TIME: _____

My Favorite Things About The Date

- [ ]
- [ ]
- [ ]
- [ ]
- [ ]
- [ ]

Email: _____

Phone: _____

_____

Address: _____

_____

What did we do?

_____

_____

_____

_____

Where Did we Go?

_____

_____

_____

_____

How Much Did I Spend?

_____

_____

_____

Things We Talked About

_____

_____

_____

How Much Did my Date Spend?

_____

_____

_____

My Screw Ups

_____

_____

My Date's Screw Ups

_____

_____

Conversation from 1-10　　1　2　3　4　5　6　7　8　9　10

KISSING?

IF YES

○ Bad Kisser

○ Mediocre Kisser

○ Good Kisser

NO ○

SEX?

IF YES, WHERE?

○ My Place

○ My Date's Place

○ Somewhere Else

NO ○

HOW WAS THE DATE?

○ Never Again

○ Awkward

○ I've Had Better

○ Nice

○ Off the Charts

○ Love at First Sight

Ideas For Next Date?

_____

_____

My Intentions

_____

_____

Notes

_____

_____

_____

My Date with _____

DATE: _____   TIME: _____

My Favorite Things About The Date

☐

☐

☐

☐

☐

☐

Email: _____

Phone: _____
_____

Address: _____
_____

What did we do?
_____
_____
_____

Where Did we Go?
_____
_____
_____

How Much Did I Spend?
_____
_____

Things We Talked About
_____
_____
_____

How Much Did my Date Spend?
_____
_____

My Screw Ups
_____
_____

My Date's Screw Ups
_____
_____

Conversation from 1-10   1 2 3 4 5 6 7 8 9 10

❯—♡—❮ KISSING? ❯—♡—❮

IF YES

○ Bad Kisser

○ Mediocre Kisser

○ Good Kisser

NO ○

❯—♡—❮ SEX? ❯—♡—❮

IF YES, WHERE?

○ My Place

○ My Date's Place

○ Somewhere Else

NO ○

HOW WAS THE DATE?

○ Never Again

○ Awkward

○ I've Had Better

○ Nice

○ Off the Charts

○ Love at First Sight

❯—♡—❮

Ideas For Next Date?

_____

_____

My Intentions

_____

_____

Notes

_____

_____

_____

My Date with _____

DATE: _____   TIME: _____

My Favorite Things About The Date

☐

☐

☐

☐

☐

☐

Email: _____

Phone: _____

_____

Address: _____

_____

What did we do?

_____

_____

_____

_____

Where Did we Go?

_____

_____

_____

_____

How Much Did I Spend?

_____

_____

_____

Things We Talked About

_____

_____

_____

How Much Did my Date Spend?

_____

_____

_____

My Screw Ups

_____

_____

My Date's Screw Ups

_____

_____

Conversation from 1-10   1 2 3 4 5 6 7 8 9 10

KISSING?

IF YES

- ○ Bad Kisser
- ○ Mediocre Kisser
- ○ Good Kisser

NO ○

SEX?

IF YES, WHERE?

- ○ My Place
- ○ My Date's Place
- ○ Somewhere Else

NO ○

HOW WAS THE DATE?

- ○ Never Again
- ○ Awkward
- ○ I've Had Better

- ○ Nice
- ○ Off the Charts
- ○ Love at First Sight

Ideas For Next Date?

_____

_____

My Intentions

_____

_____

Notes

_____

_____

_____

_____

My Date with _____

DATE: _____   TIME: _____

My Favorite Things About The Date

- ☐
- ☐
- ☐
- ☐
- ☐
- ☐

Email: _____

Phone: _____

Address: _____
_____

What did we do?
_____
_____
_____
_____

Where Did we Go?
_____
_____
_____
_____

How Much Did I Spend?
_____
_____
_____

Things We Talked About
_____
_____
_____

How Much Did my Date Spend?
_____
_____
_____

My Screw Ups
_____
_____

My Date's Screw Ups
_____
_____

Conversation from 1-10   1   2   3   4   5   6   7   8   9   10

KISSING?

IF YES

○ Bad Kisser

○ Mediocre Kisser

○ Good Kisser

NO ○

SEX?

IF YES, WHERE?

○ My Place

○ My Date's Place

○ Somewhere Else

NO ○

HOW WAS THE DATE?

○ Never Again

○ Awkward

○ I've Had Better

○ Nice

○ Off the Charts

○ Love at First Sight

Ideas For Next Date?

_____

_____

My Intentions

_____

_____

Notes

_____

_____

_____

My Date with _____

DATE: _____   TIME: _____

My Favorite Things About The Date

☐

☐

☐

☐

☐

☐

Email: _____

Phone: _____

Address: _____
_____

What did we do?
_____
_____
_____
_____

Where Did we Go?
_____
_____
_____

How Much Did I Spend?
_____
_____
_____

Things We Talked About
_____
_____
_____

How Much Did my Date Spend?
_____
_____
_____

My Screw Ups
_____
_____

My Date's Screw Ups
_____
_____

Conversation from 1-10   1   2   3   4   5   6   7   8   9   10

KISSING?

IF YES

○ Bad Kisser

○ Mediocre Kisser

○ Good Kisser

NO ○

SEX?

IF YES, WHERE?

○ My Place

○ My Date's Place

○ Somewhere Else

NO ○

HOW WAS THE DATE?

○ Never Again

○ Awkward

○ I've Had Better

○ Nice

○ Off the Charts

○ Love at First Sight

Ideas For Next Date?

_____

_____

My Intentions

_____

_____

Notes

_____

_____

_____

My Date with _____

DATE: _____   TIME: _____

My Favorite Things About The Date

☐

☐

☐

☐

☐

☐

Email: _____

Phone: _____

Address: _____
_____

What did we do?
_____
_____
_____
_____

Where Did we Go?
_____
_____
_____
_____

How Much Did I Spend?
_____
_____
_____

Things We Talked About
_____
_____
_____

How Much Did my Date Spend?
_____
_____
_____

My Screw Ups
_____
_____

My Date's Screw Ups
_____
_____

Conversation from 1-10   1   2   3   4   5   6   7   8   9   10

KISSING?

IF YES

O Bad Kisser

O Mediocre Kisser

O Good Kisser

NO O

SEX?

IF YES, WHERE?

O My Place

O My Date's Place

O Somewhere Else

NO O

HOW WAS THE DATE?

O Never Again

O Awkward

O I've Had Better

O Nice

O Off the Charts

O Love at First Sight

Ideas For Next Date?

_____

_____

My Intentions

_____

_____

Notes

_____

_____

_____

_____

My Date with _____

DATE: _____   TIME: _____

My Favorite Things About The Date

- ☐
- ☐
- ☐
- ☐
- ☐
- ☐

Email: _____

Phone: _____

Address: _____
_____

What did we do?
_____
_____
_____
_____

Where Did we Go?
_____
_____
_____
_____

How Much Did I Spend?
_____
_____
_____

Things We Talked About
_____
_____
_____

How Much Did my Date Spend?
_____
_____
_____

My Screw Ups
_____
_____

My Date's Screw Ups
_____
_____

Conversation from 1-10   1 2 3 4 5 6 7 8 9 10

KISSING?

IF YES
- ◯ Bad Kisser
- ◯ Mediocre Kisser
- ◯ Good Kisser

NO ◯

SEX?

IF YES, WHERE?
- ◯ My Place
- ◯ My Date's Place
- ◯ Somewhere Else

NO ◯

HOW WAS THE DATE?

- ◯ Never Again
- ◯ Awkward
- ◯ I've Had Better

- ◯ Nice
- ◯ Off the Charts
- ◯ Love at First Sight

Ideas For Next Date?

_____

_____

My Intentions

_____

Notes

_____

_____

_____

My Date with _____

DATE: _____　　　TIME: _____

My Favorite Things About The Date

☐

☐

☐

☐

☐

☐

Email: _____

Phone: _____

Address: _____
_____

What did we do?
_____
_____
_____
_____

Where Did we Go?
_____
_____
_____
_____

How Much Did I Spend?
_____
_____
_____

Things We Talked About
_____
_____
_____

How Much Did my Date Spend?
_____
_____

My Screw Ups
_____
_____

My Date's Screw Ups
_____
_____

Conversation from 1-10   1 2 3 4 5 6 7 8 9 10

KISSING?

IF YES

○ Bad Kisser

○ Mediocre Kisser

○ Good Kisser

NO ○

SEX?

IF YES, WHERE?

○ My Place

○ My Date's Place

○ Somewhere Else

NO ○

HOW WAS THE DATE?

○ Never Again

○ Awkward

○ I've Had Better

○ Nice

○ Off the Charts

○ Love at First Sight

Ideas For Next Date?

My Intentions

Notes

My Date with _____

DATE: _____   TIME: _____

My Favorite Things About The Date

☐

☐

☐

☐

☐

☐

Email: _____

Phone: _____

_____

Address: _____

_____

What did we do?

_____
_____
_____
_____

Where Did we Go?

_____
_____
_____
_____

How Much Did I Spend?

_____
_____
_____

Things We Talked About

_____
_____
_____

How Much Did my Date Spend?

_____
_____
_____

My Screw Ups

_____
_____

My Date's Screw Ups

_____
_____

Conversation from 1-10   1 2 3 4 5 6 7 8 9 10

KISSING?

IF YES

O Bad Kisser

O Mediocre Kisser

O Good Kisser

NO O

SEX?

IF YES, WHERE?

O My Place

O My Date's Place

O Somewhere Else

NO O

HOW WAS THE DATE?

O Never Again

O Awkward

O I've Had Better

O Nice

O Off the Charts

O Love at First Sight

Ideas For Next Date?

My Intentions

Notes

My Date with _____

DATE: _____   TIME: _____

My Favorite Things About The Date

☐

☐

☐

☐

☐

☐

Email: _____

Phone: _____

Address: _____
_____

What did we do?
_____
_____
_____
_____

Where Did we Go?
_____
_____
_____

How Much Did I Spend?
_____
_____
_____

Things We Talked About
_____
_____
_____

How Much Did my Date Spend?
_____
_____
_____

My Screw Ups
_____
_____

My Date's Screw Ups
_____
_____

Conversation from 1-10   1   2   3   4   5   6   7   8   9   10

KISSING?

IF YES
- ◯ Bad Kisser
- ◯ Mediocre Kisser
- ◯ Good Kisser

NO ◯

SEX?

IF YES, WHERE?
- ◯ My Place
- ◯ My Date's Place
- ◯ Somewhere Else

NO ◯

HOW WAS THE DATE?

- ◯ Never Again
- ◯ Awkward
- ◯ I've Had Better

- ◯ Nice
- ◯ Off the Charts
- ◯ Love at First Sight

Ideas For Next Date?

_____

_____

My Intentions

_____

Notes

_____

_____

_____

My Date with _____

DATE: _____   TIME: _____

My Favorite Things About The Date

- ☐
- ☐
- ☐
- ☐
- ☐
- ☐

Email: _____

Phone: _____

Address: _____
_____

What did we do?
_____
_____
_____
_____

Where Did we Go?
_____
_____
_____

How Much Did I Spend?
_____
_____

Things We Talked About
_____
_____
_____

How Much Did my Date Spend?
_____
_____

My Screw Ups
_____
_____

My Date's Screw Ups
_____
_____

Conversation from 1-10   1   2   3   4   5   6   7   8   9   10

KISSING?

IF YES
○ Bad Kisser
○ Mediocre Kisser
○ Good Kisser

NO ○

SEX?

IF YES, WHERE?
○ My Place
○ My Date's Place
○ Somewhere Else

NO ○

HOW WAS THE DATE?

○ Never Again
○ Awkward
○ I've Had Better

○ Nice
○ Off the Charts
○ Love at First Sight

Ideas For Next Date?

_____

_____

My Intentions

_____

_____

Notes

_____

_____

_____

My Date with _____

DATE: _____   TIME: _____

My Favorite Things About The Date

- [ ]
- [ ]
- [ ]
- [ ]
- [ ]
- [ ]

Email: _____

Phone: _____

Address: _____
_____

What did we do?
_____
_____
_____
_____

Where Did we Go?
_____
_____
_____
_____

How Much Did I Spend?
_____
_____
_____

Things We Talked About
_____
_____
_____

How Much Did my Date Spend?
_____
_____
_____

My Screw Ups
_____
_____

My Date's Screw Ups
_____
_____

Conversation from 1-10   1 2 3 4 5 6 7 8 9 10

KISSING?

IF YES
- ⭕ Bad Kisser
- ⭕ Mediocre Kisser
- ⭕ Good Kisser

NO ⭕

SEX?

IF YES, WHERE?
- ⭕ My Place
- ⭕ My Date's Place
- ⭕ Somewhere Else

NO ⭕

HOW WAS THE DATE?

- ⭕ Never Again
- ⭕ Awkward
- ⭕ I've Had Better

- ⭕ Nice
- ⭕ Off the Charts
- ⭕ Love at First Sight

Ideas For Next Date?

_____

_____

My Intentions

_____

Notes

_____

_____

_____

My Date with _____

DATE: _____ TIME: _____

My Favorite Things About The Date

☐

☐

☐

☐

☐

☐

Email: _____

Phone: _____

Address: _____
_____

What did we do?
_____
_____
_____
_____

Where Did we Go?
_____
_____
_____
_____

How Much Did I Spend?
_____
_____
_____

Things We Talked About
_____
_____
_____

How Much Did my Date Spend?
_____
_____
_____

My Screw Ups
_____
_____

My Date's Screw Ups
_____
_____

Conversation from 1-10   1 2 3 4 5 6 7 8 9 10

KISSING?

IF YES
- ◯ Bad Kisser
- ◯ Mediocre Kisser
- ◯ Good Kisser

NO ◯

SEX?

IF YES, WHERE?
- ◯ My Place
- ◯ My Date's Place
- ◯ Somewhere Else

NO ◯

HOW WAS THE DATE?

- ◯ Never Again
- ◯ Awkward
- ◯ I've Had Better

- ◯ Nice
- ◯ Off the Charts
- ◯ Love at First Sight

Ideas For Next Date?

My Intentions

Notes

My Date with _____

DATE: _____ TIME: _____

My Favorite Things About The Date

☐

☐

☐

☐

☐

☐

Email: _____

Phone: _____

Address: _____
_____

What did we do?
_____
_____
_____
_____

Where Did we Go?
_____
_____
_____
_____

How Much Did I Spend?
_____
_____
_____

Things We Talked About
_____
_____
_____

How Much Did my Date Spend?
_____
_____

My Screw Ups
_____
_____

My Date's Screw Ups
_____
_____

Conversation from 1-10   1 2 3 4 5 6 7 8 9 10

KISSING?

IF YES

NO ○

○ Bad Kisser

○ Mediocre Kisser

○ Good Kisser

SEX?

IF YES, WHERE?

NO ○

○ My Place

○ My Date's Place

○ Somewhere Else

HOW WAS THE DATE?

○ Never Again   ○ Nice

○ Awkward   ○ Off the Charts

○ I've Had Better   ○ Love at First Sight

Ideas For Next Date?

My Intentions

Notes

My Date with _____

DATE: _____   TIME: _____

My Favorite Things About The Date

☐

☐

☐

☐

☐

☐

Things We Talked About

_____
_____
_____

Email: _____
Phone: _____

Address: _____
_____

What did we do?
_____
_____
_____
_____

Where Did we Go?
_____
_____
_____

How Much Did I Spend?
_____
_____
_____

How Much Did my Date Spend?
_____
_____

My Screw Ups
_____
_____

My Date's Screw Ups
_____
_____

Conversation from 1-10   1 2 3 4 5 6 7 8 9 10

KISSING?

IF YES

○ Bad Kisser

○ Mediocre Kisser

○ Good Kisser

NO ○

SEX?

IF YES, WHERE?

○ My Place

○ My Date's Place

○ Somewhere Else

NO ○

HOW WAS THE DATE?

○ Never Again

○ Awkward

○ I've Had Better

○ Nice

○ Off the Charts

○ Love at First Sight

Ideas For Next Date?

_____

_____

My Intentions

_____

_____

Notes

_____

_____

_____

My Date with _____

DATE: _____　　　　TIME: _____

My Favorite Things About The Date

☐

☐

☐

☐

☐

☐

Email: _____

Phone: _____

Address: _____
_____

What did we do?
_____
_____
_____

Where Did we Go?
_____
_____
_____

How Much Did I Spend?
_____
_____
_____

Things We Talked About
_____
_____
_____

How Much Did my Date Spend?
_____
_____
_____

My Screw Ups
_____
_____

My Date's Screw Ups
_____
_____

Conversation from 1-10　　1　2　3　4　5　6　7　8　9　10

KISSING?

IF YES

◯ Bad Kisser

◯ Mediocre Kisser

◯ Good Kisser

NO ◯

SEX?

IF YES, WHERE?

◯ My Place

◯ My Date's Place

◯ Somewhere Else

NO ◯

HOW WAS THE DATE?

◯ Never Again

◯ Awkward

◯ I've Had Better

◯ Nice

◯ Off the Charts

◯ Love at First Sight

Ideas For Next Date?

My Intentions

Notes

My Date with _____

DATE: _____   TIME: _____

My Favorite Things About The Date

☐

☐

☐

☐

☐

☐

Email: _____

Phone: _____

Address: _____
_____

What did we do?
_____
_____
_____

Where Did we Go?
_____
_____
_____
_____

How Much Did I Spend?
_____
_____

Things We Talked About
_____
_____
_____

How Much Did my Date Spend?
_____
_____
_____

My Screw Ups
_____
_____

My Date's Screw Ups
_____
_____

Conversation from 1-10   1 2 3 4 5 6 7 8 9 10

KISSING?

IF YES
- ◯ Bad Kisser
- ◯ Mediocre Kisser
- ◯ Good Kisser

NO ◯

SEX?

IF YES, WHERE?
- ◯ My Place
- ◯ My Date's Place
- ◯ Somewhere Else

NO ◯

HOW WAS THE DATE?

- ◯ Never Again
- ◯ Awkward
- ◯ I've Had Better

- ◯ Nice
- ◯ Off the Charts
- ◯ Love at First Sight

Ideas For Next Date?

_____

_____

My Intentions

_____

_____

Notes

_____

_____

_____

My Date with _____

DATE: _____   TIME: _____

My Favorite Things About The Date

- [ ]
- [ ]
- [ ]
- [ ]
- [ ]
- [ ]

Email: _____

Phone: _____

Address: _____
_____

What did we do?
_____
_____
_____
_____

Where Did we Go?
_____
_____
_____

How Much Did I Spend?
_____
_____

Things We Talked About
_____
_____
_____

How Much Did my Date Spend?
_____
_____

My Screw Ups
_____
_____

My Date's Screw Ups
_____
_____

Conversation from 1-10   1 2 3 4 5 6 7 8 9 10

KISSING?

IF YES
- ◯ Bad Kisser
- ◯ Mediocre Kisser
- ◯ Good Kisser

NO ◯

SEX?

IF YES, WHERE?
- ◯ My Place
- ◯ My Date's Place
- ◯ Somewhere Else

NO ◯

HOW WAS THE DATE?

- ◯ Never Again
- ◯ Awkward
- ◯ I've Had Better

- ◯ Nice
- ◯ Off the Charts
- ◯ Love at First Sight

Ideas For Next Date?

_____

_____

My Intentions

_____

_____

Notes

_____

_____

_____

My Date with _____

DATE: _____   TIME: _____

My Favorite Things About The Date

- [ ]
- [ ]
- [ ]
- [ ]
- [ ]
- [ ]

Email: _____

Phone: _____

Address: _____
_____

What did we do?
_____
_____
_____
_____

Where Did we Go?
_____
_____
_____
_____

How Much Did I Spend?
_____
_____
_____

Things We Talked About
_____
_____
_____

How Much Did my Date Spend?
_____
_____
_____

My Screw Ups
_____
_____

My Date's Screw Ups
_____
_____

Conversation from 1-10   1 2 3 4 5 6 7 8 9 10

KISSING?

IF YES

- ◯ Bad Kisser
- ◯ Mediocre Kisser
- ◯ Good Kisser

NO ◯

SEX?

IF YES, WHERE?

- ◯ My Place
- ◯ My Date's Place
- ◯ Somewhere Else

NO ◯

HOW WAS THE DATE?

- ◯ Never Again
- ◯ Awkward
- ◯ I've Had Better

- ◯ Nice
- ◯ Off the Charts
- ◯ Love at First Sight

Ideas For Next Date?

My Intentions

Notes

My Date with _____

DATE: _____   TIME: _____

My Favorite Things About The Date

☐ _____

☐ _____

☐ _____

☐ _____

☐ _____

☐ _____

Email: _____

Phone: _____

Address: _____
_____

What did we do?
_____
_____
_____
_____

Where Did we Go?
_____
_____
_____
_____

How Much Did I Spend?
_____
_____

Things We Talked About
_____
_____
_____

How Much Did my Date Spend?
_____
_____

My Screw Ups
_____
_____

My Date's Screw Ups
_____
_____

Conversation from 1-10   1   2   3   4   5   6   7   8   9   10

KISSING?

IF YES

○ Bad Kisser

○ Mediocre Kisser

○ Good Kisser

NO ○

SEX?

IF YES, WHERE?

○ My Place

○ My Date's Place

○ Somewhere Else

NO ○

HOW WAS THE DATE?

○ Never Again

○ Awkward

○ I've Had Better

○ Nice

○ Off the Charts

○ Love at First Sight

Ideas For Next Date?

_____

_____

My Intentions

_____

_____

Notes

_____

_____

_____

My Date with _____

D A T E : _____ T I M E : _____

My Favorite Things About The Date

☐

☐

☐

☐

☐

☐

Email: _____

Phone: _____

Address: _____
_____

What did we do?
_____
_____
_____

Where Did we Go?
_____
_____
_____

How Much Did I Spend?
_____
_____
_____

Things We Talked About
_____
_____
_____

How Much Did my Date Spend?
_____
_____

My Screw Ups
_____
_____

My Date's Screw Ups
_____
_____

Conversation from 1-10   1   2   3   4   5   6   7   8   9   10

KISSING?

IF YES

- ◯ Bad Kisser
- ◯ Mediocre Kisser
- ◯ Good Kisser

NO ◯

SEX?

IF YES, WHERE?

- ◯ My Place
- ◯ My Date's Place
- ◯ Somewhere Else

NO ◯

HOW WAS THE DATE?

- ◯ Never Again
- ◯ Awkward
- ◯ I've Had Better

- ◯ Nice
- ◯ Off the Charts
- ◯ Love at First Sight

Ideas For Next Date?

_____

_____

My Intentions

_____

_____

Notes

_____

_____

_____

My Date with _____

DATE: _____   TIME: _____

My Favorite Things About The Date

- ☐
- ☐
- ☐
- ☐
- ☐
- ☐

Email: _____

Phone: _____

Address: _____
_____

What did we do?
_____
_____
_____
_____

Where Did we Go?
_____
_____
_____

How Much Did I Spend?
_____
_____

Things We Talked About
_____
_____
_____

How Much Did my Date Spend?
_____
_____

My Screw Ups
_____
_____

My Date's Screw Ups
_____
_____

Conversation from 1-10   1   2   3   4   5   6   7   8   9   10

KISSING?

IF YES

- ◯ Bad Kisser
- ◯ Mediocre Kisser
- ◯ Good Kisser

NO ◯

SEX?

IF YES, WHERE?

- ◯ My Place
- ◯ My Date's Place
- ◯ Somewhere Else

NO ◯

HOW WAS THE DATE?

- ◯ Never Again
- ◯ Awkward
- ◯ I've Had Better

- ◯ Nice
- ◯ Off the Charts
- ◯ Love at First Sight

Ideas For Next Date?

_____

_____

My Intentions

_____

_____

Notes

_____

_____

_____

My Date with _____

DATE: _____   TIME: _____

My Favorite Things About The Date

☐

☐

☐

☐

☐

☐

Email: _____

Phone: _____
_____

Address: _____
_____

What did we do?
_____
_____
_____
_____

Where Did we Go?
_____
_____
_____
_____

How Much Did I Spend?
_____
_____
_____

Things We Talked About
_____
_____
_____

How Much Did my Date Spend?
_____
_____
_____

My Screw Ups
_____
_____

My Date's Screw Ups
_____
_____

Conversation from 1-10   1   2   3   4   5   6   7   8   9   10

▶———♡———◀ KISSING? ▶———♡———◀

IF YES   NO ○

○ Bad Kisser

○ Mediocre Kisser

○ Good Kisser

▶———♡———◀ SEX? ▶———♡———◀

IF YES, WHERE?   NO ○

○ My Place

○ My Date's Place

○ Somewhere Else

HOW WAS THE DATE?

○ Never Again   ○ Nice

○ Awkward   ○ Off the Charts

○ I've Had Better   ○ Love at First Sight

▶———♡———◀

Ideas For Next Date?

_____

_____

My Intentions

_____

_____

Notes

_____

_____

_____

_____

My Date with _____

DATE: _____   TIME: _____

My Favorite Things About The Date

- [ ]
- [ ]
- [ ]
- [ ]
- [ ]
- [ ]

Email: _____

Phone: _____

Address: _____
_____

What did we do?
_____
_____
_____
_____

Where Did we Go?
_____
_____
_____

How Much Did I Spend?
_____
_____

Things We Talked About
_____
_____
_____

How Much Did my Date Spend?
_____
_____

My Screw Ups
_____
_____

My Date's Screw Ups
_____
_____

Conversation from 1-10   1   2   3   4   5   6   7   8   9   10

KISSING?

IF YES

○ Bad Kisser

○ Mediocre Kisser

○ Good Kisser

NO ○

SEX?

IF YES, WHERE?

○ My Place

○ My Date's Place

○ Somewhere Else

NO ○

HOW WAS THE DATE?

○ Never Again

○ Awkward

○ I've Had Better

○ Nice

○ Off the Charts

○ Love at First Sight

Ideas For Next Date?

_____

_____

My Intentions

_____

_____

Notes

_____

_____

_____

My Date with _____

DATE: _____   TIME: _____

My Favorite Things About The Date

- [ ]
- [ ]
- [ ]
- [ ]
- [ ]
- [ ]

Email: _____
Phone: _____

Address: _____

What did we do?
_____
_____
_____
_____

Where Did we Go?
_____
_____
_____

How Much Did I Spend?
_____
_____
_____

Things We Talked About
_____
_____
_____

How Much Did my Date Spend?
_____
_____

My Screw Ups
_____
_____

My Date's Screw Ups
_____
_____

Conversation from 1-10   1   2   3   4   5   6   7   8   9   10

KISSING?

IF YES
- ◯ Bad Kisser
- ◯ Mediocre Kisser
- ◯ Good Kisser

NO ◯

SEX?

IF YES, WHERE?
- ◯ My Place
- ◯ My Date's Place
- ◯ Somewhere Else

NO ◯

HOW WAS THE DATE?

- ◯ Never Again
- ◯ Awkward
- ◯ I've Had Better

- ◯ Nice
- ◯ Off the Charts
- ◯ Love at First Sight

Ideas For Next Date?

My Intentions

Notes

My Date with _____

DATE: _____   TIME: _____

My Favorite Things About The Date

- [ ]
- [ ]
- [ ]
- [ ]
- [ ]
- [ ]

Email: _____

Phone: _____

Address: _____

_____

What did we do?

_____
_____
_____
_____

Where Did we Go?

_____
_____
_____
_____

How Much Did I Spend?

_____
_____
_____

Things We Talked About

_____
_____
_____

How Much Did my Date Spend?

_____
_____
_____

My Screw Ups

_____
_____

My Date's Screw Ups

_____
_____

Conversation from 1-10   1   2   3   4   5   6   7   8   9   10

KISSING?

IF YES

○ Bad Kisser

○ Mediocre Kisser

○ Good Kisser

NO ○

SEX?

IF YES, WHERE?

○ My Place

○ My Date's Place

○ Somewhere Else

NO ○

HOW WAS THE DATE?

○ Never Again

○ Awkward

○ I've Had Better

○ Nice

○ Off the Charts

○ Love at First Sight

Ideas For Next Date?

_____

_____

My Intentions

_____

_____

Notes

_____

_____

_____

My Date with _____

DATE: _____   TIME: _____

My Favorite Things About The Date

☐

☐

☐

☐

☐

☐

Email: _____

Phone: _____

Address: _____
_____

What did we do?
_____
_____
_____

Where Did we Go?
_____
_____
_____

How Much Did I Spend?
_____
_____

Things We Talked About
_____
_____
_____

How Much Did my Date Spend?
_____
_____
_____

My Screw Ups
_____
_____

My Date's Screw Ups
_____
_____

Conversation from 1-10   1 2 3 4 5 6 7 8 9 10

KISSING?

IF YES

○ Bad Kisser

○ Mediocre Kisser

○ Good Kisser

NO ○

SEX?

IF YES, WHERE?

○ My Place

○ My Date's Place

○ Somewhere Else

NO ○

HOW WAS THE DATE?

○ Never Again   ○ Nice

○ Awkward   ○ Off the Charts

○ I've Had Better   ○ Love at First Sight

Ideas For Next Date?

My Intentions

Notes

My Date with _____

DATE: _____   TIME: _____

My Favorite Things About The Date

☐

☐

☐

☐

☐

☐

Email: _____
Phone: _____

Address: _____
_____

What did we do?
_____
_____
_____

Where Did we Go?
_____
_____
_____
_____

How Much Did I Spend?
_____
_____
_____

Things We Talked About
_____
_____
_____

How Much Did my Date Spend?
_____
_____

My Screw Ups
_____
_____

My Date's Screw Ups
_____
_____

Conversation from 1-10   1 2 3 4 5 6 7 8 9 10

KISSING?

IF YES

○ Bad Kisser

○ Mediocre Kisser

○ Good Kisser

NO ○

SEX?

IF YES, WHERE?

○ My Place

○ My Date's Place

○ Somewhere Else

NO ○

HOW WAS THE DATE?

○ Never Again

○ Awkward

○ I've Had Better

○ Nice

○ Off the Charts

○ Love at First Sight

Ideas For Next Date?

My Intentions

Notes

My Date with _____

DATE: _____   TIME: _____

My Favorite Things About The Date

☐

☐

☐

☐

☐

☐

Email: _____

Phone: _____

Address: _____
_____

What did we do?
_____
_____
_____

Where Did we Go?
_____
_____
_____

How Much Did I Spend?
_____
_____
_____

Things We Talked About
_____
_____
_____

How Much Did my Date Spend?
_____
_____

My Screw Ups
_____
_____

My Date's Screw Ups
_____
_____

Conversation from 1-10   1 2 3 4 5 6 7 8 9 10

KISSING?

IF YES
- ◯ Bad Kisser
- ◯ Mediocre Kisser
- ◯ Good Kisser

NO ◯

SEX?

IF YES, WHERE?
- ◯ My Place
- ◯ My Date's Place
- ◯ Somewhere Else

NO ◯

HOW WAS THE DATE?

- ◯ Never Again
- ◯ Awkward
- ◯ I've Had Better

- ◯ Nice
- ◯ Off the Charts
- ◯ Love at First Sight

Ideas For Next Date?

_____

_____

My Intentions

_____

Notes

_____

_____

_____

My Date with _____

DATE: _____   TIME: _____

My Favorite Things About The Date

☐

☐

☐

☐

☐

☐

Email: _____

Phone: _____

Address: _____
_____

What did we do?
_____
_____
_____
_____

Where Did we Go?
_____
_____
_____

How Much Did I Spend?
_____
_____

Things We Talked About
_____
_____
_____

How Much Did my Date Spend?
_____
_____

My Screw Ups
_____
_____

My Date's Screw Ups
_____
_____

Conversation from 1-10   1 2 3 4 5 6 7 8 9 10

KISSING?

IF YES

○ Bad Kisser

○ Mediocre Kisser

○ Good Kisser

NO ○

SEX?

IF YES, WHERE?

○ My Place

○ My Date's Place

○ Somewhere Else

NO ○

HOW WAS THE DATE?

○ Never Again

○ Awkward

○ I've Had Better

○ Nice

○ Off the Charts

○ Love at First Sight

Ideas For Next Date?

My Intentions

Notes

My Date with _____

DATE: _____   TIME: _____

My Favorite Things About The Date

☐

☐

☐

☐

☐

☐

Email: _____

Phone: _____

Address: _____
_____

What did we do?
_____
_____
_____

Where Did we Go?
_____
_____
_____

How Much Did I Spend?
_____
_____
_____

Things We Talked About
_____
_____
_____

How Much Did my Date Spend?
_____
_____

My Screw Ups
_____
_____

My Date's Screw Ups
_____
_____

Conversation from 1-10   1   2   3   4   5   6   7   8   9   10

KISSING?

IF YES

○ Bad Kisser

○ Mediocre Kisser

○ Good Kisser

NO ○

SEX?

IF YES, WHERE?

○ My Place

○ My Date's Place

○ Somewhere Else

NO ○

HOW WAS THE DATE?

○ Never Again

○ Awkward

○ I've Had Better

○ Nice

○ Off the Charts

○ Love at First Sight

Ideas For Next Date?

My Intentions

Notes

My Date with _____

DATE: _____   TIME: _____

My Favorite Things About The Date

☐

☐

☐

☐

☐

☐

Email: _____

Phone: _____

Address: _____
_____

What did we do?
_____
_____
_____

Where Did we Go?
_____
_____
_____
_____

How Much Did I Spend?
_____
_____

Things We Talked About
_____
_____
_____

How Much Did my Date Spend?
_____
_____
_____

My Screw Ups
_____
_____

My Date's Screw Ups
_____
_____

Conversation from 1-10   1   2   3   4   5   6   7   8   9   10

KISSING?

IF YES
- ◯ Bad Kisser
- ◯ Mediocre Kisser
- ◯ Good Kisser

NO ◯

SEX?

IF YES, WHERE?
- ◯ My Place
- ◯ My Date's Place
- ◯ Somewhere Else

NO ◯

HOW WAS THE DATE?

- ◯ Never Again
- ◯ Awkward
- ◯ I've Had Better

- ◯ Nice
- ◯ Off the Charts
- ◯ Love at First Sight

Ideas For Next Date?

My Intentions

Notes

My Date with _____

DATE: TIME:

My Favorite Things About The Date

- [ ]
- [ ]
- [ ]
- [ ]
- [ ]
- [ ]

Email: _____

Phone: _____

Address: _____
_____

What did we do?
_____
_____
_____

Where Did we Go?
_____
_____
_____
_____

How Much Did I Spend?
_____
_____
_____

Things We Talked About
_____
_____
_____

How Much Did my Date Spend?
_____
_____
_____

My Screw Ups
_____
_____

My Date's Screw Ups
_____
_____

Conversation from 1-10   1   2   3   4   5   6   7   8   9   10

KISSING?

IF YES

- ⃝ Bad Kisser
- ⃝ Mediocre Kisser
- ⃝ Good Kisser

NO ⃝

SEX?

IF YES, WHERE?

- ⃝ My Place
- ⃝ My Date's Place
- ⃝ Somewhere Else

NO ⃝

HOW WAS THE DATE?

- ⃝ Never Again
- ⃝ Awkward
- ⃝ I've Had Better

- ⃝ Nice
- ⃝ Off the Charts
- ⃝ Love at First Sight

Ideas For Next Date?

My Intentions

Notes

My Date with _____

DATE: _____ TIME: _____

My Favorite Things About The Date

- [ ]
- [ ]
- [ ]
- [ ]
- [ ]
- [ ]

Email: _____

Phone: _____

Address: _____

What did we do?

_____

_____

_____

Where Did we Go?

_____

_____

_____

How Much Did I Spend?

_____

_____

_____

Things We Talked About

_____

_____

_____

How Much Did my Date Spend?

_____

_____

_____

My Screw Ups

_____

_____

My Date's Screw Ups

_____

_____

Conversation from 1-10   1 2 3 4 5 6 7 8 9 10

KISSING?

IF YES
- ◯ Bad Kisser
- ◯ Mediocre Kisser
- ◯ Good Kisser

NO ◯

SEX?

IF YES, WHERE?
- ◯ My Place
- ◯ My Date's Place
- ◯ Somewhere Else

NO ◯

HOW WAS THE DATE?

- ◯ Never Again
- ◯ Awkward
- ◯ I've Had Better

- ◯ Nice
- ◯ Off the Charts
- ◯ Love at First Sight

Ideas For Next Date?

_____

_____

My Intentions

_____

_____

Notes

_____

_____

_____

My Date with _____

DATE: _____

TIME: _____

My Favorite Things About The Date

☐

☐

☐

☐

☐

☐

Email: _____

Phone: _____

Address: _____
_____

What did we do?
_____
_____
_____
_____

Where Did we Go?
_____
_____
_____
_____

How Much Did I Spend?
_____
_____
_____

Things We Talked About
_____
_____
_____

How Much Did my Date Spend?
_____
_____

My Screw Ups
_____
_____

My Date's Screw Ups
_____
_____

Conversation from 1-10   1 2 3 4 5 6 7 8 9 10

KISSING?

IF YES
- ○ Bad Kisser
- ○ Mediocre Kisser
- ○ Good Kisser

NO ○

SEX?

IF YES, WHERE?
- ○ My Place
- ○ My Date's Place
- ○ Somewhere Else

NO ○

HOW WAS THE DATE?

- ○ Never Again
- ○ Awkward
- ○ I've Had Better

- ○ Nice
- ○ Off the Charts
- ○ Love at First Sight

Ideas For Next Date?

_____

_____

My Intentions

_____

_____

Notes

_____

_____

_____

_____

My Date with _____

DATE: _____   TIME: _____

My Favorite Things About The Date

☐

☐

☐

☐

☐

☐

Email: _____

Phone: _____

Address: _____
_____

What did we do?
_____
_____
_____

Where Did we Go?
_____
_____
_____

How Much Did I Spend?
_____
_____
_____

Things We Talked About
_____
_____
_____

How Much Did my Date Spend?
_____
_____

My Screw Ups
_____
_____

My Date's Screw Ups
_____
_____

Conversation from 1-10   1   2   3   4   5   6   7   8   9   10

KISSING?

IF YES

O Bad Kisser

O Mediocre Kisser

O Good Kisser

NO O

SEX?

IF YES, WHERE?

O My Place

O My Date's Place

O Somewhere Else

NO O

HOW WAS THE DATE?

O Never Again

O Awkward

O I've Had Better

O Nice

O Off the Charts

O Love at First Sight

Ideas For Next Date?

My Intentions

Notes

My Date with _____

DATE: _____   TIME: _____

My Favorite Things About The Date

- ☐
- ☐
- ☐
- ☐
- ☐
- ☐

Email: _____

Phone: _____

Address: _____
_____

What did we do?
_____
_____
_____

Where Did we Go?
_____
_____
_____

How Much Did I Spend?
_____
_____

Things We Talked About
_____
_____
_____

How Much Did my Date Spend?
_____
_____

My Screw Ups
_____
_____

My Date's Screw Ups
_____
_____

Conversation from 1-10   1   2   3   4   5   6   7   8   9   10

KISSING?

IF YES
- ◯ Bad Kisser
- ◯ Mediocre Kisser
- ◯ Good Kisser

NO ◯

SEX?

IF YES, WHERE?
- ◯ My Place
- ◯ My Date's Place
- ◯ Somewhere Else

NO ◯

HOW WAS THE DATE?

- ◯ Never Again
- ◯ Awkward
- ◯ I've Had Better

- ◯ Nice
- ◯ Off the Charts
- ◯ Love at First Sight

Ideas For Next Date?

My Intentions

Notes

My Date with _____

DATE: _____　　TIME: _____

My Favorite Things About The Date

- [ ]
- [ ]
- [ ]
- [ ]
- [ ]
- [ ]

Email: _____

Phone: _____

Address: _____
_____

What did we do?
_____
_____
_____

Where Did we Go?
_____
_____
_____

How Much Did I Spend?
_____
_____

Things We Talked About
_____
_____
_____

How Much Did my Date Spend?
_____
_____

My Screw Ups
_____
_____

My Date's Screw Ups
_____
_____

Conversation from 1-10　　1　2　3　4　5　6　7　8　9　10

KISSING?

IF YES

○ Bad Kisser

○ Mediocre Kisser

○ Good Kisser

NO ○

SEX?

IF YES, WHERE?

○ My Place

○ My Date's Place

○ Somewhere Else

NO ○

HOW WAS THE DATE?

○ Never Again

○ Awkward

○ I've Had Better

○ Nice

○ Off the Charts

○ Love at First Sight

Ideas For Next Date?

My Intentions

Notes

My Date with _____

DATE: _____   TIME: _____

My Favorite Things About The Date

☐

☐

☐

☐

☐

☐

Email: _____

Phone: _____

Address: _____
_____

What did we do?
_____
_____
_____
_____

Where Did we Go?
_____
_____
_____

How Much Did I Spend?
_____
_____

Things We Talked About
_____
_____
_____

How Much Did my Date Spend?
_____
_____

My Screw Ups
_____
_____

My Date's Screw Ups
_____
_____

Conversation from 1-10   1 2 3 4 5 6 7 8 9 10

KISSING?

IF YES
- ○ Bad Kisser
- ○ Mediocre Kisser
- ○ Good Kisser

NO ○

SEX?

IF YES, WHERE?
- ○ My Place
- ○ My Date's Place
- ○ Somewhere Else

NO ○

HOW WAS THE DATE?

- ○ Never Again
- ○ Awkward
- ○ I've Had Better

- ○ Nice
- ○ Off the Charts
- ○ Love at First Sight

Ideas For Next Date?

My Intentions

Notes

My Date with _____

DATE: _____   TIME: _____

My Favorite Things About The Date

- [ ]
- [ ]
- [ ]
- [ ]
- [ ]
- [ ]

Email: _____

Phone: _____

Address: _____
_____

What did we do?
_____
_____
_____
_____

Where Did we Go?
_____
_____
_____

How Much Did I Spend?
_____
_____
_____

Things We Talked About
_____
_____
_____

How Much Did my Date Spend?
_____
_____

My Screw Ups
_____
_____

My Date's Screw Ups
_____
_____

Conversation from 1-10   1 2 3 4 5 6 7 8 9 10

KISSING?

IF YES

- ◯ Bad Kisser
- ◯ Mediocre Kisser
- ◯ Good Kisser

NO ◯

SEX?

IF YES, WHERE?

- ◯ My Place
- ◯ My Date's Place
- ◯ Somewhere Else

NO ◯

HOW WAS THE DATE?

- ◯ Never Again
- ◯ Awkward
- ◯ I've Had Better

- ◯ Nice
- ◯ Off the Charts
- ◯ Love at First Sight

Ideas For Next Date?

My Intentions

Notes

My Date with _____

DATE: _____   TIME: _____

My Favorite Things About The Date

☐ _____

☐ _____

☐ _____

☐ _____

☐ _____

☐ _____

Email: _____

Phone: _____

Address: _____
_____

What did we do?
_____
_____
_____

Where Did we Go?
_____
_____
_____

How Much Did I Spend?
_____
_____
_____

Things We Talked About
_____
_____
_____

How Much Did my Date Spend?
_____
_____

My Screw Ups
_____
_____

My Date's Screw Ups
_____
_____

Conversation from 1-10   1 2 3 4 5 6 7 8 9 10

KISSING?

IF YES
- ◯ Bad Kisser
- ◯ Mediocre Kisser
- ◯ Good Kisser

NO ◯

SEX?

IF YES, WHERE?
- ◯ My Place
- ◯ My Date's Place
- ◯ Somewhere Else

NO ◯

HOW WAS THE DATE?

- ◯ Never Again
- ◯ Awkward
- ◯ I've Had Better

- ◯ Nice
- ◯ Off the Charts
- ◯ Love at First Sight

Ideas For Next Date?

My Intentions

Notes

My Date with _____

DATE: _____   TIME: _____

My Favorite Things About The Date

- ☐
- ☐
- ☐
- ☐
- ☐
- ☐

Email: _____

Phone: _____

Address: _____
_____

What did we do?
_____
_____
_____
_____

Where Did we Go?
_____
_____
_____
_____

How Much Did I Spend?
_____
_____
_____

Things We Talked About
_____
_____
_____

How Much Did my Date Spend?
_____
_____
_____

My Screw Ups
_____
_____

My Date's Screw Ups
_____
_____

Conversation from 1-10   1   2   3   4   5   6   7   8   9   10

KISSING?

IF YES
- ⭕ Bad Kisser
- ⭕ Mediocre Kisser
- ⭕ Good Kisser

NO ⭕

SEX?

IF YES, WHERE?
- ⭕ My Place
- ⭕ My Date's Place
- ⭕ Somewhere Else

NO ⭕

HOW WAS THE DATE?

- ⭕ Never Again
- ⭕ Awkward
- ⭕ I've Had Better

- ⭕ Nice
- ⭕ Off the Charts
- ⭕ Love at First Sight

Ideas For Next Date?

My Intentions

Notes

My Date with _____

DATE: _____   TIME: _____

My Favorite Things About The Date

- [ ]
- [ ]
- [ ]
- [ ]
- [ ]
- [ ]

Email: _____
Phone: _____

Address: _____
_____

What did we do?
_____
_____
_____
_____

Where Did we Go?
_____
_____
_____
_____

How Much Did I Spend?
_____
_____
_____

Things We Talked About
_____
_____
_____

How Much Did my Date Spend?
_____
_____
_____

My Screw Ups
_____
_____

My Date's Screw Ups
_____
_____

Conversation from 1-10   1 2 3 4 5 6 7 8 9 10

KISSING?

IF YES

○ Bad Kisser

○ Mediocre Kisser

○ Good Kisser

NO ○

SEX?

IF YES, WHERE?

○ My Place

○ My Date's Place

○ Somewhere Else

NO ○

HOW WAS THE DATE?

○ Never Again

○ Awkward

○ I've Had Better

○ Nice

○ Off the Charts

○ Love at First Sight

Ideas For Next Date?

My Intentions

Notes

My Date with _____

DATE: _____   TIME: _____

My Favorite Things About The Date

- [ ]
- [ ]
- [ ]
- [ ]
- [ ]
- [ ]

Email: _____

Phone: _____

Address: _____
_____

What did we do?
_____
_____
_____
_____

Where Did we Go?
_____
_____
_____
_____

How Much Did I Spend?
_____
_____
_____

Things We Talked About
_____
_____
_____

How Much Did my Date Spend?
_____
_____
_____

My Screw Ups
_____
_____

My Date's Screw Ups
_____
_____

Conversation from 1-10   1 2 3 4 5 6 7 8 9 10

KISSING?

IF YES
- ⭕ Bad Kisser
- ⭕ Mediocre Kisser
- ⭕ Good Kisser

NO ⭕

SEX?

IF YES, WHERE?
- ⭕ My Place
- ⭕ My Date's Place
- ⭕ Somewhere Else

NO ⭕

HOW WAS THE DATE?

- ⭕ Never Again
- ⭕ Awkward
- ⭕ I've Had Better

- ⭕ Nice
- ⭕ Off the Charts
- ⭕ Love at First Sight

Ideas For Next Date?

_____

_____

My Intentions

_____

Notes

_____

_____

_____

My Date with _____

DATE: _____   TIME: _____

My Favorite Things About The Date

☐

☐

☐

☐

☐

☐

Email: _____

Phone: _____

Address: _____

_____

What did we do?
_____
_____
_____

Where Did we Go?
_____
_____
_____
_____

How Much Did I Spend?
_____
_____

Things We Talked About
_____
_____
_____

How Much Did my Date Spend?
_____
_____

My Screw Ups
_____
_____

My Date's Screw Ups
_____
_____

Conversation from 1-10   1 2 3 4 5 6 7 8 9 10

KISSING?

IF YES

O Bad Kisser

O Mediocre Kisser

O Good Kisser

NO O

SEX?

IF YES, WHERE?

O My Place

O My Date's Place

O Somewhere Else

NO O

HOW WAS THE DATE?

O Never Again

O Awkward

O I've Had Better

O Nice

O Off the Charts

O Love at First Sight

Ideas For Next Date?

_____

_____

My Intentions

_____

Notes

_____

_____

_____

My Date with _____

DATE: _____   TIME: _____

My Favorite Things About The Date

☐ _____

☐ _____

☐ _____

☐ _____

☐ _____

☐ _____

Email: _____

Phone: _____

Address: _____

_____

What did we do?

_____

_____

_____

_____

Where Did we Go?

_____

_____

_____

How Much Did I Spend?

_____

_____

_____

Things We Talked About

_____

_____

_____

How Much Did my Date Spend?

_____

_____

My Screw Ups

_____

_____

My Date's Screw Ups

_____

_____

Conversation from 1-10   1 2 3 4 5 6 7 8 9 10

KISSING?

IF YES

○ Bad Kisser

○ Mediocre Kisser

○ Good Kisser

NO ○

SEX?

IF YES, WHERE?

○ My Place

○ My Date's Place

○ Somewhere Else

NO ○

HOW WAS THE DATE?

○ Never Again

○ Awkward

○ I've Had Better

○ Nice

○ Off the Charts

○ Love at First Sight

Ideas For Next Date?

My Intentions

Notes

My Date with _____

DATE: _____   TIME: _____

My Favorite Things About The Date

☐

☐

☐

☐

☐

☐

Email: _____
Phone: _____

Address: _____
_____

What did we do?
_____
_____
_____
_____

Where Did we Go?
_____
_____
_____
_____

How Much Did I Spend?
_____
_____

Things We Talked About
_____
_____
_____

How Much Did my Date Spend?
_____
_____

My Screw Ups
_____
_____

My Date's Screw Ups
_____
_____

Conversation from 1-10   1 2 3 4 5 6 7 8 9 10

KISSING?

IF YES

○ Bad Kisser

○ Mediocre Kisser

○ Good Kisser

NO ○

SEX?

IF YES, WHERE?

○ My Place

○ My Date's Place

○ Somewhere Else

NO ○

HOW WAS THE DATE?

○ Never Again

○ Awkward

○ I've Had Better

○ Nice

○ Off the Charts

○ Love at First Sight

Ideas For Next Date?

_____

_____

My Intentions

_____

_____

Notes

_____

_____

_____

My Date with _____

DATE: _____   TIME: _____

My Favorite Things About The Date

- ☐
- ☐
- ☐
- ☐
- ☐
- ☐

Email: _____

Phone: _____

Address: _____
_____

What did we do?
_____
_____
_____

Where Did we Go?
_____
_____
_____
_____

How Much Did I Spend?
_____
_____
_____

Things We Talked About
_____
_____
_____

How Much Did my Date Spend?
_____
_____

My Screw Ups
_____
_____

My Date's Screw Ups
_____
_____

Conversation from 1-10   1 2 3 4 5 6 7 8 9 10

KISSING?

IF YES
- ◯ Bad Kisser
- ◯ Mediocre Kisser
- ◯ Good Kisser

NO ◯

SEX?

IF YES, WHERE?
- ◯ My Place
- ◯ My Date's Place
- ◯ Somewhere Else

NO ◯

HOW WAS THE DATE?

- ◯ Never Again
- ◯ Awkward
- ◯ I've Had Better

- ◯ Nice
- ◯ Off the Charts
- ◯ Love at First Sight

Ideas For Next Date?

My Intentions

Notes

My Date with _____

DATE: _____ TIME: _____

My Favorite Things About The Date

☐

☐

☐

☐

☐

☐

Email: _____

Phone: _____

Address: _____
_____

What did we do?
_____
_____
_____
_____

Where Did we Go?
_____
_____
_____

How Much Did I Spend?
_____
_____
_____

Things We Talked About
_____
_____
_____

How Much Did my Date Spend?
_____
_____
_____

My Screw Ups
_____
_____

My Date's Screw Ups
_____
_____

Conversation from 1-10   1 2 3 4 5 6 7 8 9 10

KISSING?

IF YES

◯ Bad Kisser

◯ Mediocre Kisser

◯ Good Kisser

NO ◯

SEX?

IF YES, WHERE?

◯ My Place

◯ My Date's Place

◯ Somewhere Else

NO ◯

HOW WAS THE DATE?

◯ Never Again

◯ Awkward

◯ I've Had Better

◯ Nice

◯ Off the Charts

◯ Love at First Sight

Ideas For Next Date?

My Intentions

Notes

My Date with _____

DATE: _____   TIME: _____

My Favorite Things About The Date

☐

☐

☐

☐

☐

☐

Email: _____

Phone: _____

Address: _____
_____

What did we do?
_____
_____
_____
_____

Where Did we Go?
_____
_____
_____
_____

How Much Did I Spend?
_____
_____
_____

Things We Talked About
_____
_____
_____

How Much Did my Date Spend?
_____
_____
_____

My Screw Ups
_____
_____

My Date's Screw Ups
_____
_____

Conversation from 1-10   1 2 3 4 5 6 7 8 9 10

KISSING?

IF YES
- ◯ Bad Kisser
- ◯ Mediocre Kisser
- ◯ Good Kisser

NO ◯

SEX?

IF YES, WHERE?
- ◯ My Place
- ◯ My Date's Place
- ◯ Somewhere Else

NO ◯

HOW WAS THE DATE?

- ◯ Never Again
- ◯ Awkward
- ◯ I've Had Better

- ◯ Nice
- ◯ Off the Charts
- ◯ Love at First Sight

Ideas For Next Date?

_____

_____

My Intentions

_____

_____

Notes

_____

_____

_____

My Date with _____

DATE: _____   TIME: _____

My Favorite Things About The Date

- ☐ _____
- ☐ _____
- ☐ _____
- ☐ _____
- ☐ _____
- ☐ _____

Email: _____

Phone: _____

Address: _____
_____

What did we do?
_____
_____
_____

Where Did we Go?
_____
_____
_____

How Much Did I Spend?
_____
_____
_____

Things We Talked About
_____
_____
_____

How Much Did my Date Spend?
_____
_____

My Screw Ups
_____
_____

My Date's Screw Ups
_____
_____

Conversation from 1-10   1   2   3   4   5   6   7   8   9   10

KISSING?

IF YES

○ Bad Kisser

○ Mediocre Kisser

○ Good Kisser

NO ○

SEX?

IF YES, WHERE?

○ My Place

○ My Date's Place

○ Somewhere Else

NO ○

HOW WAS THE DATE?

○ Never Again   ○ Nice

○ Awkward   ○ Off the Charts

○ I've Had Better   ○ Love at First Sight

Ideas For Next Date?

_____

_____

My Intentions

_____

_____

Notes

_____

_____

_____

_____

My Date with _____

DATE: _____   TIME: _____

My Favorite Things About The Date

☐

☐

☐

☐

☐

☐

Email: _____

Phone: _____

Address: _____
_____

What did we do?
_____
_____
_____
_____

Where Did we Go?
_____
_____
_____
_____

How Much Did I Spend?
_____
_____

Things We Talked About
_____
_____
_____

How Much Did my Date Spend?
_____
_____
_____

My Screw Ups
_____
_____

My Date's Screw Ups
_____
_____

Conversation from 1-10   1   2   3   4   5   6   7   8   9   10